## THE GEORGIA POETRY PRIZE

The University of Georgia Press established
the Georgia Poetry Prize in 2016 in partnership
with the Georgia Institute of Technology,
Georgia State University, and the University of
Georgia. The prize is supported by the Bruce and
Georgia McEver Fund for the Arts and Environment.

# A BODY OF WATER

# A BODY
# OF WATER

CHIOMA URAMA

The University of Georgia Press

Athens

"Tryna Get Right with God" originally appeared in *Prairie Schooner*.
"Blue" and *"poli—"* first appeared in *Blackbird*, and "Skraw" in the *Lindenwood Review*.

© 2021 by the University of Georgia Press
Athens, Georgia 30602
www.ugapress.org
All rights reserved
Designed by Rebecca A. Norton
Set in 11/16 Garamond Premier Pro
Printed and bound by Sheridan Books, Inc.
The paper in this book meets the guidelines for
permanence and durability of the Committee on
Production Guidelines for Book Longevity of the
Council on Library Resources.

Most University of Georgia Press titles are
available from popular e-book vendors.

Printed in the United States of America
25  24  23  22  21  P  5  4  3  2  1

Library of Congress Control Number: 2020946232
ISBN: 9780820358574 (paperback)
ISBN: 9780820358581 (ebook)

for Barbara and Lionel
and all the Blues in between

You know, they straightened out the Mississippi River in places, to make room for houses and livable acreage. Occasionally the river floods these places. "Floods" is the word they use, but in fact it is not flooding; it is remembering. Remembering where it used to be. All water has a perfect memory and is forever trying to get back to where it was.

—TONI MORRISON

# CONTENTS

## BRIDE

## GROOM

## WITNESS

# BRIDE

Bride: Barbara Ann Gardner
Age: 15
Race: Colored
Single, Widowed, Divorced: Single
No. Times Prev. Married: None
Occupation: None
Birthplace: Wilson, N.C.
Father's Full Name: Wheeler Gardner
Mother's Maiden Name: Gertrude Hayes
Proposed Date of Marriage: February 20th, 1958

~~Worten~~

---

~~Best~~
~~Gardner~~
~~Gardner~~
~~Gardner~~
~~Gardner~~
~~Blue~~
Urama

Isac Worten (1818) and Danah Worten (1820) begat _____, who begat their grandson John William Best (1867). John William begat Florence (1889), who married Quincy (1887) and became a Gardner. Florence and Quincy had eight children, the eldest being Wheeler (1909), who married Gertrude Hayes (1901). Wheeler and Gertrude had Beatrice (1927) and then her daughter Barbara Ann (1943), who they would raise and claim as their own.

## GOOGLE SEARCH FOR MY ANCESTOR "JOHN BEST," "PLANTATION," AND "NORTH CAROLINA"

16 **Best** South Carolina Plantations - VacationIdea.com
Tour the South's **Best** Historic Homes - Southern Living
The now restored slave quarters on the property are one of the **best** . . .

7 **Best** Places in North Carolina to Take Mom for Mother's Day
Brunch
This *plantation* is one of the **best** in the Lowcountry
Guided tours are available, but this *plantation* is best taken in by . . .

**Best** Attractions and Activities for Visitors and Locals Alike
Plantations to Tour in Eastern North Carolina | Getaway USA
We were very grateful for her efforts and felt this was the **best** tour we
had ever . . .

Which *plantation* is **best** in Charleston?
Here you'll discover the **best** of both worlds—
The *plantation* raised beans, corn and peas but was perhaps **best**-known
for its . . .

# A 70% PROBABILITY THAT YOU WILL HAVE THE SAME ATTACHMENT STYLE AS YOUR MOTHER (OR, SIX GENERATIONS REMOVED FROM ENSLAVEMENT)

go away

go away

go away

go away

go away

go away

come here, go away

come here, go away

come here, go away

come here, go away

come here, go away

come here, go away

come

         away

     go

here

# VERY USED QUEEN-SIZED MATTRESS

Free for whoever
come and take it—very used
Queen mattress.
No calls please.
Will take this down
as soon as it's gone.

# THE FUTURE AS WRITTEN BY 16-YEAR-OLD GIRLS

i.

this is your relationship to the subject:

ii.

black umbrella (pleather)
stringy hair
a woman petting herself

iii.

your feelings exist on another side of the room

iv.

You are 12. The man you are having sex with is 21.

    doing it this way is important to you

v.

nose wide open
dripping love

vi.

There's no such thing as disembodied dick.

vii.

He puts his hand on the small of your back and steers you through the
dinner party. His fingers inside you as if you were a doll.

viii.

as if you are not at all human

ix.

you are held together with bits of rope

x.

*STOP. skip. skip. PLAY:*

xi.

the warm violence of moonlight
the thinning sycamore trees
the sliding balcony door

xii.

a reflection of you            (a glass argument)
a lyrical father

xiii.

you accommodate the loneliness that moves into your body

xiv.

it stalks within you like a cat, chews on your insides, slops out in a
tangle into the bucket

xv.

your daughter spills into the room, and it is you on another plane, you
in some altered universe beneath a wall of water

xvi.

she is a doll, living in a corner of yourself, eating moonlight

xvii.
a lyric

xviii.
she gravitates toward a man who will put his hand on her

xix.
warm violence

xx.
they fuck in her mother's bed

xxi.
this is important to her

xxii.
disembodied

xxiii.
she is a sliding door

xxiv.
a thinning tree

xxv.
glass

xxvi.
nose wide open
dripping

## AS TOLD BY 16-YEAR-OLD GIRLS

I got out the shower, and he was doing pushups
on the floor. Niggas are so fucking weird.

I felt him trying to pull my shorts to the side, trying to
reach inside me without me noticing

his face like he got caught doing something

My grandma told me horror stories about that
before I was even old enough to have sex.

He came everywhere. I had heard cum can stay
alive outside the body for 3 or 4 days.

Then he would swear it's not his.

That's what he meant by the lion
in the cage; he was tryna trap me.

How to fuck up a black girl's day:

Insert two fingers wet with okra juice.
Or, swallow four cups of oregano tea.

Someone handed me a pamphlet.
Someone put on a video about not letting men touch you,

but by then it was too late.

The thing about her baby daddy is
she talked to him about an abortion.

At the very last minute, he changes his mind.
Like, wow, you're just an asshole.

He swore it wasn't his.

She walked around for weeks
bleeding

## A WINDOWLESS ROOM

You set up tent in
my throat, then built
a fire

She pulls down her collar
to show you the mark

last winter I was soaping my
ten-year-old cousin's legs in the
bath and I realized that they
were mine

Remember?
Remember how they were?
How much they wanted?

some part of me already
chosen to continue on autonomously

if we can predict it
we can carve it out
with a spoon and swallow

last winter I was soaping my
legs and I realized that they
were mine

She is sitting in a windowless
room
I repeat her name
as if to summon a god

I am making her immortal

*how often do you talk to your*
*mother*, I ask
some part of me on
fire

I pull from her spoon
and swallow

she's dead, she says,
soaping the mark,
tenting her legs,
summoning a window
carved for a god,
remember?

.⸴

.

i.

my mother doodles large ballpoint eyes
on the back of a bill. Flowers for flower's
sake. Triangles to trap it all down.

it seemed that youth had never happened
to them. There is nothing you can do
about this.

the face gets blacker
+ blacker

next to her birdcages, my great-great-
grandmother sets aside a stack of children's
coloring books for herself.

those who survive it always have such
romantic stories about being poor.

street energies

my sister scrawls a forest of shapes into her
forearm. Her face hovers in a grimace
inches above the tree line.

hindsight permits this kind of erasure.
There is nothing you can do about this.


ii.

What if happiness feels superhuman?


iii.

my aunty lives alone / her bedroom as
sensitive as a shrine / in the basement
is a locked room full of dolls / so
clean and white / it has become difficult
to enter


iv.

I'll call this one, "Water stains on metro
pass."


v.

in her journal my youngest sister
proclaims, "I am alone,"
and then,
"No one understands."


vi.

you are reacting the way you would.

## SUDDENLY, IT'S DUSK

*I feel most colored when I am thrown against a sharp white background.*
When I am with my family, I have no gender or race (the weight of all
that). No age. There is no time, the river of years sluicing up against the
smooth bank of the present. The yellow pat of sun melts into the trees;
the birds row away to their nests. Take what meaning you will. I can't
wait to tell somebody "no" to something.

A basin to wash the delicates in. She never cared much about the
work; it was as if she was somewhere else. "It doesn't matter if I like it;
it matters that you feel it." Pure gold. I would have let that little boy
comb me bald I loved him so much I love him so much. How humbling
to wake up in a pool of your own blood. A button nose. The incessant
chatter of the television. There is a God who's listening. "Fix your face"
means to arrange it in an order so that it's not conveying what's on the
inside.

The day we first had sex, I wore a tie-dye navy blue dress with printed
seashells that was my mother's, bought on the first vacation we ever
took to Virginia Beach when I was nine, a trip so spontaneous I wasn't
sure we would be returning—this wasn't the first time she'd threatened
abandoning my father, there had been several shelters full of battered,
watercolored women—but then, at the end of the third day, we piled
in the car and went back home. My family is full of petite women, but
the dress my mother had drowned in was tight on me in all the right
places, not to mention cotton, and I was mad with you, but I remember
forgetting when I put that dress on.

The prehistoric wail of geese. Brightly painted abandoned cages. Something grey and round and soft like an emu. Dragonflies swatting through the air. Lizards rustling through the fallen leaves. Chicken hawks tethered to the wind. Water bugs ripple across the surface of the pond. A group of female peacocks taking so much effort to lift themselves into the arms of the banyan, squawking, cooing like doves. Grey fruit. The sun melting. Something all alone whooping on the other side of the trees, and not a single thing calling back to it.

fiddle leaf fig        golden coconuts spoiled in the palm's cradle        the blue tarp swollen with wind        ivy crawling up the siding; scales        the satisfying crunch of seeds    a street that breaks in the middle like a stream before resuming again

*What kind of writer are you?* A black one. The crow in the branch warns the one in the street picking at the tattered remains of a squirrel. The procession of geese moves further into the field that is slowly becoming a pond. *What genre is that?* A house glowing like a jack-o'-lantern through the trees. A tipped safety cone. The bench dripping mist. *What do black girls have to say?* Sirens echo off the brick schoolhouse. The field quivers beneath fingers of wind. The geese jump up and row away.

I've never known
a Christmas, but
my mother's favorite
Christmas gift was a dictionary.
When I ask her why,
she replies,
"It's a book full of words,"
as if the glory of lending
name to experience
is all there is

## TRYNA GET RIGHT WITH GOD

She crawls around in others' emotions all day, trying them on and
  sobbing.

She sits in a room with the radio going, going ships sinking, unnatural
  disasters, form over content—speak it.

They say, "the black body," and she can smell the burnt basement bulb
  swinging on its cord, a black girl in a blue dress lying in a pile of
  rust-colored leaves, George Washington's wide-toothed Igbo grin.

At 8:15 p.m. she will write, The conditions for peace are already present.

She can remember sharing a desk in grade school with a white boy
  who spoke incessantly, like he might explode if he didn't. She can
  remember stabbing him in the face with the point of her pencil.
  She would never do anything like that now.

Someone's bending back the finger on the hand of a very small child
  who refuses to cry.

False flowers, she will say to her son when he calls, you ever heard of
  anything more offensive?

She believes that the mushroom that bloomed at the base of her pot of
  devil's ivy is a miracle.

At 7:30 a.m. she will write, DO NOT COVET.

There is a notebook full of torn recipes from soup can labels and advice
from talk shows: *free yourself through validation. Yes, I can hear
you screaming, hips.*

She will tune in to the sounds of her neighbors relaxing into their
Saturday.

She holds the blunt end of a knife toward the yolk of an avocado. Light
pours into the room like a slowly forming idea. Today, she exists in
the most sensible corner of a dream. She can't remember who she's
wearing.

## SO WILDLY BAD (BLUE-BLACK GIRL)

She was the party
She shaped like jelly all over
She smiles (an embarrassed child)
She turns her head

# GROOM

Groom: Lionel Blue
Age: 19
Race: Colored
Single, Widowed, Divorced: Single
No. Times Prev. Married: None
Occupation: Laborer
Birthplace: Rocky Mount, N.C.
Father's Full Name: John Blue
Mother's Maiden Name: Mary Jones
Proposed Date of Marriage: February 20th, 1958

Benjamin Blue (1879) and Mattie Blue (1881) begat John Blue (1902). John married Olivia (1903), whose parents were David Vaughn (1880) and Molisha Dean (?). Oliva and John begat John Jr. (?) and Clifton (?)—who were both drafted in WWII—and Mary (1919). Mary begat Lionell (1937) in Rocky Mount, North Carolina.

LIONEL BLUE AS ACCORDING TO U.S. CENSUS DATA
(OR, MANY U.S. SCHOOLS TAUGHT SPELLING BY
PHONICS; OR, THE SPELLING OF A NAME WAS UP
TO THE CENSUS TAKER; OR, YOUR GRANDFATHER'S
PEOPLE WERE NEVER TAUGHT TO READ)

Lionel Blue
Lionnel Blue
Lionell T. Blue
Lonnel Blue

# SKRAW

(n.)

pronunciation:[1] /skrô/

1.  the coarse pseudonym for hay; fodder
    for feeding, material especially for weaving

2.  Black children open up their mouths and somebody's grandparent
    tumbles out, *Thank you, baby. Don't eem worry 'bout it.* There are
    no silly geese for them, no lucky ducks, no gilded infantilization of
    a childhood as fragile as a golden egg.
    a.  I'm watching a group of second graders argue over who
        will turn next—insults made magnificent through claps
        and pointing—when I notice her standing next to me.
        Holding the straps of the bright pink backpack over her
        shoulders in her fists, she squints through the cream-
        colored hair barrettes dangling in her face, "Do you know
        that when you sign somebody else's name on a piece of

---

[1] Pronunciation similar to "scrawl," similar to letters sprawling all over the page,
that kindergarten language that we are taught to edit out of ourselves through
aligning the text left, starting at the top, and making our way down to the
somewhere. I had the fifth- and sixth-grade girls for an hour of creative writing
during summer camp each day, and the only way to get them to cooperate was to
put them in the Everglades. *It's day 3. You've lost all your supplies in the rainstorm,
and you can't find your way back to camp.* Inexplicably, they made a way out of no
way, slicing the heads off of alligators, eating panther raw before wearing it. They
mumbled apologies to lizards, then swallowed them whole while fighting through
torrents of rain. They hid in the reeds under swollen blue moons and wrote their
stories down on the beach in shark teeth and seashells for the helicopters circling
above: *I AM HUNGRY AND I AM TIRED BUT I AM ALIVE.*

paper, it's called forgery?" She rocks back and forth on her toes. "My mama told me that." From then on, I would call her the forgerist but to everyone else she was Kay Kay or Kanariyah, a name like some beautiful strange kind of bird. She was six, a rising first grader with a face so chubby and perfectly round that I sketched it for her twice. Twice, she took a black crayon and scribbled out her eyes, her nose, her mouth, until she was satisfied with her complete obliteration.

b. For linguists, accessing the historical documentation of African American speech has always been problematic. The difficulties are compounded for vernacular speech that has been deemed unworthy of preservation by society.

3. something of little or no value, trifle

a. Technically, it wasn't a curse word, but it was light enough to be hurled across the playground like one. *Jit!* They spit it in each other's faces and smiled slyly at me before running. Technically, it wasn't a curse word. Admittedly, I had no idea what it meant. They broke it down: *It's like a little kid, like you being childish.* Pejorative, U.S. prison slang, an inexperienced, foolhardy young man. *Jit can't even hold a ball . . .*

b. A child's world is ripe with gore. They slip up and their precious little faces burst open. They cry for the jewels of blood spilt all over the blacktop. They are constantly faced with their own mortality, which has the effect of making them more dangerous, more brave, more sensible than any of us.

c. The trouble was that words as they experienced them existed in a different reality than words on the page. The widening chasm between the auditory and visual made reading and writing difficult and logically impractical. The natural response of many of the kindergarteners was frustration followed by dismissal.

3.  a single dried stalk of grain, a particle
        of multifarious use
    of essence


Origins: black, specifically, American Black, that southern blue-black
vernacular warm as a mango-colored bruise; related to the issue we
Africans
will always have wit dem "*t's*"
where "*str*" becomes a hard swift "*k*"
think: skrong, and skruggle, and skreet
        *Deskroy her*!
a flick of the tongue
just enough to change linguistic
course of direction


Sentence: *The first little pig's house was built out of skraw!*

# ROCKY MOUNT MILLS

Along the river with lots of ups and downs!

Review of **Tar River Trail**
★★★★★ Reviewed June 29, 2017

I stayed overnight at the Rocky Mount at the Candlewood Suites (an excellent hotel) and in the morning found this amazing trail which meanders along the Tar River. It snakes through the entire city. I ran 1.5 miles out from Sunset Park and back. I passed a couple of deer watching me run. Lots of birds singing in the trees. The river was flowing and the sunrise was beautiful. I never felt unsafe. This is a great place to run.

Rocky Mount is derived from the nickname Rocky Mound, after the Rocky Mound at the falls of the Tar River. This is also the site of one of the first cotton mills in North Carolina.

The construction of the original stone building in which the cotton mill was housed was begun in either 1816 or 1817. The original mill was built in 1818 and was the second cotton mill established in North Carolina.

The mill building itself was about 76 feet long by 30 feet wide. Built from local granite, the facility, housing cotton and grist mills, was three stories plus a basement.

It flourished in the decades leading up to the Civil War, when it began churning out cloth for Confederate uniforms. That, combined with its economic prominence, made it a target for Union troops, who burned down the building in 1863. The rebuilt mill was torched again in 1869 by a disgruntled worker. The present building has stood since about 1870.

The history of Rocky Mount Mills is closely interwoven with the history of one family, the BATTLE family, for it is in the hands of this one family that the fortunes of the Mills have largely rested for the past 125 years.

Slaves and a few free African Americans supplied the labor from the earliest days until about 1852, when the Battles began to substitute white workers, many of them women and children. By that time, local slaveowners were less inclined to hire their slaves out for factory work.

In its character as a community enterprise, its principal customers were the local plantation owners who brought their corn to the grist mill to be ground and their raw cotton to the cotton mill, where it was spun into yarn.

For some years prior to and during the Civil War, the mill was a general supply station for warps, which the women of the South wove into cloth on the old hand looms.

Some coarse cloth was manufactured at the mill, moreover, which was used to clothe the slave population of the surrounding plantations.

JAMES SMITH BATTLE, who with his son acquired control of Rocky Mount Mills in 1847, was one of the largest plantation owners in North Carolina. At the time of his death, he owned about 20,000 acres of rich river land especially suitable for cotton raising and was the master of some 500 slaves. At then current values, this slave holding was itself worth more than $300,000.

One incident of JAMES BATTLE's career exemplified his high standard of moral responsibility.

A slave

on his plantation became embroiled in an unfortunate quarrel with an overseer, as the result of which the overseer was stabbed by

the negro

and died. After careful investigation of the circumstances, Battle became convinced that

the slave

had acted in self-defense under extreme provocation. He therefore determined to see that

the slave

received justice. Battle thus became perhaps the first slave owner in the South to defend

a slave

in court against the charge of murder of a white man. He engaged two leading members of the North Carolina Bar to represent

the negro,

to one of whom he is reported to have paid the very substantial fee of one thousand dollars. When

the negro

was adjudged guilty in a primary court and sentenced to death, an appeal was carried to the state supreme court, which reversed the decision and saved

the man's life.

Great trail to run, however . . .

**Review of Tar River Trail**
★★★ Reviewed December 17, 2019

While the trail itself is great, the maps and directions online and in the park aren't very easy to find. The colored line painted on the paved trail to mark each section is faded and at times missing. There is one junction where the trail splits coming from Sunset Park and there is no indication as to which way to go. It was not readily identifiable where the trail was. You have to drive to the back of the park and look for the "Emergency Access Trail" sign (not sure why it is an emergency).

That the prisoner Will, was the property of James S. Battle

That the deceased, Richard Baxter, was the overseer entrusted with
management of the prisoner

That the early morning of the 22nd day of January slave Will had a
dispute with slave Allen

That slave Allen was the foreman on the same plantation who was
likewise property of said Battle

That the dispute arose surrounding a hoe

That slave Will claimed to have used this particular hoe exclusively on
the farm

That slave Will was said to have used the hoe to clear the farm in his
own time

That slave Allen did not care; assigned the work and the hoe to another
slave anyway

That slave Will broke the helve of the hoe and sent it sailing through
the air before walking off about ¼ mile to his new assignment at
the cotton screw

That slave Allen couldn't wait to run and tell overseer Baxter

That overseer Baxter immediately turned into his house for his gun

That overseer Baxter's wife, who'd been watching all of this from the
window, was heard to say, "I would not, my dear."

That overseer Baxter marched past her, replying with positive certainty,
"I will."

That overseer Baxter told slave Allen to take his cowhide and follow
him at a distance

That overseer Baxter mounted his horse and rode confidently to the
cotton screw

That overseer Baxter—without being observed by slave Will—
dismounted hastily, his gun in his hand

That overseer Baxter, with the determination of a farmer culling his
herd, drew everyone's attention as he walked directly to the box on
which slave Will was standing, throwing cotton into the press

That overseer Baxter smiled crudely and ordered slave Will to come
down

That all the work around them ceased

That, noticing the gun and Baxter's disposition, slave Will carefully
removed his own hat

That the removal of slave Will's battered straw hat was done so in efforts
to humble himself as he stood high above Baxter on the box

That slave Will lowered his eyes, then his head, toward the hat he
turned slowly in his hands

That the term that comes to mind is "genuflect"

That slave Will came down

That overseer Baxter spoke some words to slave Will that the three
negroes present would never repeat

That the negro Will made off running

That Baxter fired upon him

That all would recall that the shot was deafeningly loud

That the whole load was released into negro Will's back, creating a
wound like a crater covering a space of 12 inches square

That this alone should have proved fatal

That negro Will didn't know this, that he kept running anyway

That Baxter sent two other slaves into the fields after negro Will

That Baxter dropped his empty gun and mounted his horse saying to
slave Allen, "He could not go far."

That this belief was Baxter's undoing

That slave Allen on horse headed negro Will off in the field

That negro Will changed course for the woods

That Baxter dismounted to pursue negro Will on foot

That negro Will had run five or six hundred yards from the place he'd
been shot

That the wound in negro Will's back began to breathe, forcing him,
finally, to slow down

That Baxter came on negro Will from behind and collared him with his
right hand

That negro Will twisted and bucked away

That—at this moment—the negroes ordered to pursue negro Will
caught up to them

That a struggling Baxter shouted for the negroes to help him lay hold of
negro Will

That before anyone else could touch him, prisoner negro Will had
already gotten Baxter's left thumb between his teeth

That prisoner negro Will reached down into the waist of his pants and
drew a knife

That prisoner negro Will struck at the approaching slaves

That his aim missed and cut a writhing Baxter in the thigh

That a scuffle ensued

That prisoner negro Will nicked Baxter in the chest

That prisoner negro Will sliced Baxter above the elbow

That this was the cut that forced Baxter to let go

That prisoner negro Will breathlessly staggered off into the woods

That Baxter—stumbling to the ground bleeding—directed the negroes
to pursue him

That Baxter, changing his mind, recalled them seconds later

That the cut in Baxter's arm was four inches long and two inches deep

That the flesh lolled open like the mouth of a tired infant

That Baxter sputtered, "Will has killed me . . ." as he bled out under the
reproachful eyes of two slaves

That that evening, Will emerged from the woods, a spackled trail of his
own blood shadowed behind him

That Will went to master Battle and surrendered himself

That Will was promptly arrested and informed of overseer Baxter's
death

That an astonished Will exclaimed, "Is it possible!"

That Will appeared so much affected by the reality of such a feat that
only then did he come just short of falling

# "POLI—"

*after an untitled sketch by Basquiat*

To your right, a Crayola yellow square.
Inside this, a tiny brown car.
Outside the square, are a few distressed longitudinal lines,
Red and Black.
Below the square is the word, "*poli—* "

A square of yellow hallway light, just warm and large and fleeting enough
for the jury to pretend with them. Trick black. Black trick. Eenie,
meeny, miney, no. Naw, man. Naw, man, GET UP. GETCHO ASS
UP! !#$%....... !#$% ....... !# *THIS IS A TEST OF THE EMERGENCY
BROADCASTING SYSTEM* ....... !# !# Please do not enter history
head on. Step sideways as if you were entering Yemaya. *5-O nigga! 5-O!*
She was asleep on the couch next to her grandmother, both dressed
in a magnificent square of television light. Amber waves of grain. His
weapon fired a single shot. His shot a single fired weapon. His single shot
a fired weapon. His single weapon fired a shot. His weapon. His shot.
*Fire!* The old woman shakes. Her fists tremble in front of her face. Her
cry is Florida's trembling metronomic moan for James,

> *Damn, damn, damn!*

Inside the square: violence.
The yellow is assaulting,
systematic. A bleating caution signal.
Outside the square: distress.
The penciled half word "*poli—* "
prophetic. A fragmented warning.

If I run, you run, nigga, we all runnin. This was founded / Years ago / By broke slaves / Years ago / Who did not have / Years ago. They gathered around the computer to watch him die again and again on a loop. The bullet struck the child in the head—*But then, suddenly I knew somebody else did it, some bastard had hurt a little girl*—and exited her neck. No, it was a man at the bottom of a staircase with arms like rifles. No, it wasn't a man at all. Something inside the woman is kneeling. Chanting, "You ain't nothin but a bitch wit a badge!" The crowd was barking at them, so they hit it on the nose. The children took off through the streets with bricks, crying rivulets of milk. They fed them from an ailing river that sat down in one place like a swamp. I. Am. In. *TEARS*. This isn't a real answer. She isn't the victim we typically cry for. Wade through the stomach of the storm to fetch a bale of Wonder Bread. Thieving-ass nigga. Triflin'-ass nigga. *I was trying to stay calm*—It didn't happen. It did not happen—*but nobody would talk to me*. They kicked in the door and shot the girl in her sleep. White ppl, plz.

The square of light is tyrannical,
a cinematic announcement of the primitive
tiny brown car. Inside this,
there are bars on the windows.
The half-word scrawled below leans right, which
graphology reveals as a loss of logic.
Hysteria is close by.

*Naw, man. Naw. Please, get up. I'm begging.* In the little girl dream is a creamsicle sunset, a forest, a ring of princesses unfurling spools of golden hair to the cackling music of her braids as she dances with them. To be young, gifted, and black. And dead. It was a suicide. They pinned her eyes open with Photoshop. The hell is wrong with y'all? She's calling to her as if she were a song. *No woman, no cry*. None of it makes any sense; where is the body supposed to go? Please let him be alive. Please let him be alive. He didn't need to explain why he'd imagined it. *Y'all can't fuck wit the po-lice. Y'all can't fuck wit the po-lice.* She unhinges her jaw and sirens pour into the room. The water covered the chariots, the horsemen, and all that came into the sea after them. In the little girl dream the cry pricks a murder of crows from the trees. It is the last thing she feels before dark.

# WEIGHING COTTON

Here, we are three pictures:
they're all black lines on white ground
thick brush strokes
three of them
       Woah!
it is its own statement
all of a sudden it's dusk
we're worried about flying things
shadow pulled to the surface
color is one of the best ways to make people feel good
make a miracle so I know it's you

he said he had a child
a daughter, maybe,
out West somewhere
the idea of a baby
which was light enough
to press behind his ear
as he moved forward

*KA CHI FO!*

*I messed this day up. I'd like a new one.*

no grave, no cold marble
plaque for weeping, no glass
vase for the oddly colored
carnations no one thinks to bring

*I want more. Just . . . a third one?*

a Nigerian greets me with
excitement, trailed by
confusion,
              dismay, dismissal

*I am not going to be.*

no photographs

*This is the room I have never been in.*

*Ka chi fo!*
the only Igbo my
father ever taught me

*I was gonna ask someone else to do it.*

language petrified
by disuse

*This is the part that needs to be screamed:*

come the end of the party
throw your arms around
your relatives, recite it
as if it were song
*Ka chi fo*! *Ka chi fo*! *Ka chi fo*!
Goodnight!

*I'd like someone to hold my hand for this part.*

now, I see that he was
planning—even then—to
leave us

# MENDING IN THE PEDIATRIC WARD

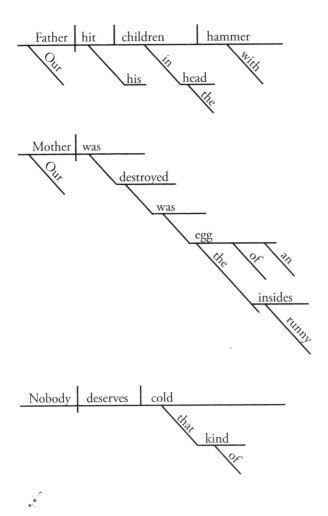

# MY GRANDMOTHER WAS IGBO

on the basement stairs,
she wraps me
in her skin.
I force a smile,
remembering
water poured on my brother and I
cold
in the bath. Her breath
rotten, she cries over me
in her language I was
taught to forget.
hard as I can
I nod

I nod
hard as I can,
taught to forget
in her language I was
rotten. She cries over me
in the bath, her breath
cold,
water poured on my brother, and I,
remembering,

I force a smile.
in her skin
she wraps me
on the basement stairs

## RECIPE FOR JOLLOF RICE

5 peppers
onion
garlic
tomato
red pepper
& blend

no measurements for any of these because it's always different; it's
always how you're wanting it

for the ultimate rice:
      dry tomato in oven
      w/ a maggi cube & wait til
      you see burnt on top & blend it

& cont. w/oil

another way: cook tomatoes down
fry in oil w/ onion (make sure onion
                is fried 1st; this is
                about the taste!)

fresh bay leaf only (if you want to make the one that will trap a
husband)
+maggi
+organic tomato paste (half can)
        (ain't nobody ever had enough tomato
        in real life)
+curry
+thyme (a lot)
+more maggi
+"bone broth"
+water

It should look like tomato soup.
     +a tiny bit of crayfish for pop

rice soaks up ~~right~~ salt (taste broth so you know how much salt you
need) you want the broth to be salty
add more maggi & salt (season until your ancestors say "STOP")
Cameroon pepper (just a dash)
when sauce is right, add rice
& more water

break the bay leaf inside
+add top
+leave on medium

watchit

# AN INISOLABLE PORTRAIT

*after Lyn Hejinian*

Summers are patterned with sharp, filtered light. No different from the flakes of sun on the skin of the pool, deceptively lavish mercurial slivers. Luna's magenta sari balloons behind her on evening walks. One of the butter containers in the fridge is packed with cold compost refuse. The trees are always hungry, carnivorous. The plaintive moans of swallows hidden in the somewhere. My brother storms the austere fortress in search of a pixeled princess. If you mean it, it would be in writing. It would move across the damp sky like white moths. It was simply a bush with a mouth like a cave. Now I remember being pulled to the bus stop each morning by the cat. Take your shoes off at the door. To reach the sink without the step stool. My mother works nights under the bright lights of a stockroom, slicing her fingers open with a box cutter. It was as if the flies never understood how angry we were with them. Open up all the windows at night so that the house can breathe; my mother believes in the curative power of pine. My father has faith in his wilting tomatoes, heat, bad soil, or no. We are deeply afraid of the raccoon rabbits. The oak tree undresses herself beneath the hard-yellow sun. If you dig a hole in the backyard, you had better fill it up before you come back in this house. We ruin the cabbage soup diet with pepperoni slices. So much of the family dinner was reaching onto the plate of the person next to you to eat something that was likely already on your own. My mother lit after my brother, chasing him with the wooden spoon as he did laps around the dining room table. Tom and Jerry come to life. If you are angry, then why is it that you are smiling? Thanksgiving turkey is eaten at eleven in the morning so that the children are sated, the rest of the day pregnant with the opportunity for second dinners. When my cricket dies, I take it out of the goldfish bowl and keep it in a ring box until it dissolves. The story goes: across the school playground lives the murder house, the murderer, the dead woman wrapped in a pile of golden leaves. We had to take it out to the porch if we were going to get loud. Stand under the awning and dip pieces of yourself into the rain. An arm, a leg, but never the head.

# BLUE

I am in love with the self-possessed scrap of Florida sky from my
occluded kitchen window—what a wonderful way to be propertied!—
and I think this is the spreading feeling my ancestor must have had
when they looked up and took the name down for themselves. You see,
I cannot think of Blue without thinking of my grandmother, without
thinking of my grandfather who I only knew through the static of
the VHS tape he sent me because he had never been taught to write.
This is the spirit with which I was poured into the world: blue was my
first language, the ink my mother bathed me in, christened blue-black
girl—my blue-black brother crying, crying. Blue is my lens; the pastoral
violence of Virginia childhood lulled to a swollen yawning innocence
when blanketed in this color. And I cannot write about blue without
writing about Billie, without writing about swaying to the coppery rust
of her voice on the patio under a broken fingernail of moon with you.

after years
of searching my father's name
he returns to me
in a Youtube sermon
petitioning the audience
to run to God

# WITNESS

# A BODY OF WATER

i.

*what star did you come from?*

ii.

the broken toilet trickling like a creek,
you clean one piece of me at a time
with your tongue in slow circles
as if you can numb selectively.
I pray for you to open my eyes,
and my heart shutters closed
witnessing the smokestack of
twilight coming on. Your eyes plead,
*be soft with me*, but I can already feel
the tide pulsing in my stomach,
clawing at the soil of my skin

## BIBLE STUDY

I kept tally of the
breaks in silence: muffled
coughs, shoes shuffling down the
aisle. A time for standing, a time
for song, a time for sitting &
pretending to listen. Learning the
backs of folks' heads, reading
the gentle nods of sleep, the violent
jump awake
      I don't know where I was then but
I was elsewhere
      during the bible stories of
King Solomon rewarding women
who would rather see
their child living with demons
than divided
while
black women have
given their children
to Yemaya, tossed them in
wells & ocean swells rather than
hand them over to white men
      for poking & prodding on
the auction block
& they were not wrong.

# JEHOVAH'S PEOPLE

What it was like to grow up
   just outside of God
& to know that you could never
   inhabit her
that Our God wasn't a "her"
but a him
a father with unrelenting hands
that there would be no hymns, no
ecstasy, no healing touch
only organized religion
wrestling my child body into
an un'natural quiet, I did not
learn discipline but I became
intimately acquainted with fear
there were people the congregation
would not talk to
   those who left the flock
people made to sit alone in the back
shrouded in shame that
we resolved by pretending
not to see
my sister said if you look at
anything long enough you
can bore holes in it
disintegrate it with laughter

or peppermint lingering on trails
of whispered voices
that person in the back row
that fallen bird
    who was once my cousin
      then my mother
who committed the terrible error
of being too much flesh
and too much fire
in a place where only God
could be both.

sometimes (frequently)
I'll abandon my body
my soul momentarily forgetting its contract of
sinew & blood & muscle
its promise to eat breathe sleep shit
      never mind the fucking
sometimes, it throws its hands up &
walks off the job mid-conversation
mid-activity (at a concert, in a grocery
store aisle)
  leaving the container
sinew blood muscle
fumbling for the ground

I try not to think about it
   the hall, the silence, the
   passionless voices
that is, I'm trying to show respect for it
   the order, the aisles, the only-men-may-
   deliver-this talks
because some part of me still believes
   the hand raising, the knee-length
   skirts, the pregnant girl sobbing,
   running into the street, the black car
   hitting its breaks
it's true

I am exhausted from the shock
   of your spirit flying from mine

I pray every day I'll lift an
elbow and a note you left me
will fall: this is only temporary

I dreamt the poem that
would save us all
a sestina of Ultramarine
children draped over a
chain-link fence
toes crushing vines flowering
over the mesh,
centipedes moving in locomotion
along subtropical pines splayed
toward the air like grasping hands
the little boy in too big overalls
skewers you with his ballpoint blue eyes,
says, *spend more time in your body*
*or someone else will*

I have the words I need to heal myself.

I have the words I need to heal myself.

I have the words I need to heal myself.

I have the words I need to heal myself.

I have the words I need to heal myself.

I have the words I need to heal myself.

I have the words I need to heal myself.

I have the words I need to heal myself.

I have the words I need to heal myself.

I have the words I need to heal myself.

I have the words I need to heal myself.

I have the words I need to heal myself.

I have the words I need to heal myself.

I have the words I need to heal myself.

I have the words I need to heal myself.

I have the words I need to heal myself.

I have the words I need to heal myself.

I have the words I need to heal myself.

a name
is a charm
or medicine (agwu)
a supplication
imploring you
to carry out
the petition
it calls

# WHAT THE CHILDREN'S NAMES MEAN

god Knows
god's Love is
a Blessing
a Gift

## CHIMA

oh baby
god knows
god knows
god knows
what he done
and she's coming
to get you

## CHIOMA

good god
god is good!
god's love,
a prayer of good luck
and favor
and you a carrier
a container for her

# NGOZI

ngozi is the blessing
extended over us
through
prayer
& ngozi
is the house
webbed with sunlight
& ngozi
is a fury of maddening
sketches
flushing us each
out of the deck
like cards
& ngozi
is the welt of anger
stretching down our throats
when the coffee table
comes down on
her finger—so much blood
it was stunning—and still
she refuses to cry

# NKECHI

nkechi
*nkem,*
who is mine
and not mine
who is ours
and never ours
god's own
—we are only
borrowers—walks
into the living room
calmly announcing
that the house
is on fire

# A LIST OF THINGS THAT GIVE ME PLEASURE (OR, REDIRECTING MY BODY TOWARD PLEASURE)

fountain pens
fingers combing through a pile of sand
the space between a lover's chin and chest
someone you love calling out to you in a crowded room
water threading through your scalp
the moon locking its eye on you
la luna como la leche y el cielo como las negritas
wearing the same smile as your grandmother
the fullness of both hands
the salt of the ocean soaking the meanness out of your skin returning
        you to soft (always this)
bathing in swollen rivers
being held by the ground beneath a tree
a little boy called June Bug
swan boats
purple kale
blood oranges
your dancing mouth
the curve of my collarbone
finding a tree to lay under
pink, purple, and gold durags
revelations in warm showers
waves swelling with moonshine
buying golden and rust-colored plantains
standing on a piece of driftwood in the moonlight

the absence of fear after letting it consume your body like fire
a deep slumber as thick as molasses
ginger tea
a stranger being the mother you need in the moment
the view of the volcano from the apartment
plants quivering beneath a waterfall
hot water and lemon
lime and watermelon
a clean bed
conversations with babies
maracuya
working from home
slivers of moments when you witness a teenager through all the
      madness of adolescence
allowing new emotions to bloom
underneath moonlight now
movement, my first love
the seducing light beyond the bridge of myself
windchime
circles
slowly

I know I hold on to a lot,
too much,
I save shopping bags and paper
boxes
I have a trunk full of recycling
and drawings coated in glitter
I turn the words I've never said
over and over in my head
until they are smooth as river stones
and
even then, I don't toss them

# THE REVOLUTION WILL NOT GO WELL WITH COKE & OTHER NOTES FROM MY GRANDMOTHER

1) the bible is a guide so much as any other self-help book
2) listen to your body
3) listen to your intuition
4) you're in more danger when you don't use your voice than when you do
5) you can't help anyone if you don't 1st help yourself
6) your imagination can create as much beauty as it does fear. meditation is a practice in quieting and strengthening your mind, the same as any muscle
7) <u>write it down</u>; let those feelings out
8) push good energy into the world
9) apologize when you've made a mistake; no matter how small, it matters to be able to admit you've learned & are growing
10) if something makes you feel strongly about it (good or bad) go more deeply into that thing
11) you are beautiful. you are powerful. remember this.
12) honor your creativity by keeping your space positive & in order
13) dance often
14) wash your hair at least every 3 weeks (like a fine cloth)
15) all of your writing is necessary. good & bad are relative & often irrelevant. ask yourself instead, does it make you jump?
16) don't be afraid to do what you need to for yourself whether its ignoring that call, telling that person the truth, cutting that person off; go with your gut

17) everything around you is comprised of energy: TV, music, images, blogs etc. you must intuit whether this energy is energy that best serves you.
18) you are created in God's image
19) you are comprised of millions of years of information. tap into it.
20) you are a sensitive spiritual person. it is in your DNA (this is a learning process).

Also! breathe into your hips
        work on opening yourself up
create a home inside yourself
paint the painting white

in the moonlight
your body something borrowed
something blue
blooms
desire now a compass
carrying us
further into dark

in the fantasy
we bump into each other out back
the scene
    blacker
+ blacker
water stains on
mercury,
envision this place,
where we speak in
minor twangs
two black strings
dragging and singing
with no need to
swallow their music,
nose wide open
and everything

when we were younger, we played on the slide in our backyard—except it wasn't a slide; it was our boat. we were on a mission to guide it to safety somewhere along the crooked fence. you howled as if your feet had been scorched by coals and called it wind, and I rocked us back and forth. we went on like that until the evening brought in a warm shade of empurpled blue that dissolves fingertips, and we were no longer troubled with floating.

# GRATITUDE

We give thanks for Stephanie Denise Urama and Ikechukwu Urama. Without the medicine of their experience this book would not be possible. We give thanks for Barbara Ann Blue for her wisdom, guidance, and protection. We give thanks to the ancestors for allowing their stories to be shared. We give thanks for Chermeca Gilchrist, who allowed us access to her DNA ancestry results, which provided the seeds for this book of record. We give thanks for Ngozi Urama for painting the cover image that brought the book to life. We give thanks for Chima and Nkechi Urama for their muse. We give thanks for Maureen Seaton for creating space, for holding space, and for sharing the magic of her existence. We give thanks for Samina Gul Ali for her endless love and consideration and for always holding me accountable. We give thanks for the support of University of Georgia Press. We give thanks for family and community in Maryland, Virginia, Miami, and New Orleans. Thank you for cocreating this reality with me.

# NOTES

The book's epigraph is from Toni Morrison's "The Sight of Memory," in *Inventing the Truth: The Art and Craft of Memoir*, 2nd edition, edited by William Zinsser (Boston; New York: Houghton Mifflin, 1995), 83–102.

Italicized sentence in "Suddenly, It's Dusk" is from the Zora Neale Hurston's *How It Feels to be Colored Me*.

"Rocky Mount Mills" is a found poem collaging language from the North Carolina Department of Natural and Cultural Resources, TripAdvisor, an article by Brian Mims in *Our State* magazine, and Nash County, NCGenWeb. Photograph reproduced with the permission of Charles Harris.

"*poli*—" borrows language from the following (in order of appearance): *Good Times* (1974), Kanye West, Charles Jones (father of Aiyana Stanley-Jones), Frank Bidart, Charles Jones, Nina Simone, Bob Marley and The Wailers, *Next Friday* (2000).

"An Inisolable Portrait" is patterned after the work of Lyn Hejinian.

## THE GEORGIA POETRY PRIZE

Christopher Salerno, *Sun & Urn*
Christopher P. Collins, *My American Night*
Rosa Lane, *Chouteau's Chalk*
Chelsea Dingman, *Through a Small Ghost*
Chioma Urama, *A Body of Water*